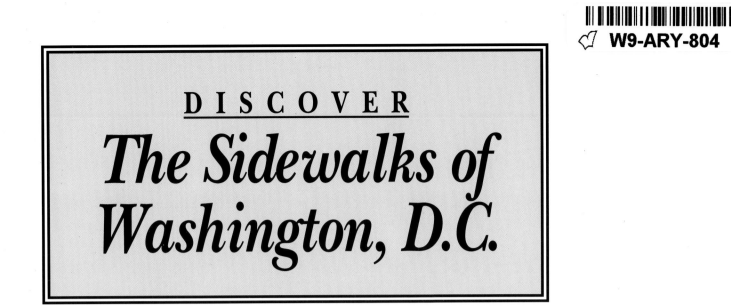

DISCOVER
The Sidewalks of Washington, D.C.

DISCOVER
The Sidewalks of Washington, D.C.

BY ROBERT SEIDENBERG

PHOTOGRAPHY BY
KEVIN VANDIVIER & JOE VIESTI

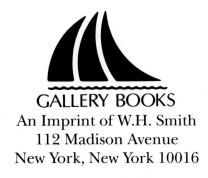

GALLERY BOOKS
An Imprint of W.H. Smith
112 Madison Avenue
New York, New York 10016

A FRIEDMAN GROUP BOOK

Published by GALLERY BOOKS
An imprint of W. H. Smith Publishers, Inc.
112 Madison Avenue
New York, New York 10016

ISBN 0-8317-9306-6

DISCOVER THE SIDEWALKS OF WASHINGTON, D.C.
was prepared and produced by
Michael Friedman Publishing Group, Inc.
15 West 26th Street
New York, New York 10010

Editor: James K. Blum
Art Director: Robert W. Kosturko
Photo Editor: Christopher C. Bain
Production Manager: Karen L. Greenberg

All photographs © Viesti Associates.
Viesti Associates is a stock-photography library
with offices in New York City and Austin, Texas.

Color separations by Hong Kong Scanner Craft Company, Ltd.
Printed and bound in Hong Kong by Leefung-Asco Printers, Ltd.

Photographs © Kevin Vandivier 1989: 9, 19, 20-21, 27, 32-33, 38, 42-43, 44, 58 (all),
60, 61, 62-63, 63 (r), 64.
Photographs © Joe Viesti 1989: 3, 8, 12 (l), 12-13, 14 (l), 14-15, 16-17, 17 (r), 22, 23,
25, 26, 28-29, 30, 31, 34,35, 36 (all), 37, 39, 40-41, 43 (r), 45, 46, 47, 50-51,
52 (l), 52 (r), 53, 54-55, 55 (r), 56, 57, 59, 65, 66, 67, 68-69, 70-71, 72 (all).

C O N T E N T S

PART ONE

Monumental Washington

PAGE 9

PART TWO

Occupational Washington

PAGE 23

PART THREE

Recreational Washington

PAGE 47

PART FOUR

Cultural Washington

PAGE 67

PART ONE

Monumental Washington

Washington, D.C. conjures images of stately white-marbled monuments even for those who have never visited the nation's capital. Founded as both a seat of government and a showplace, Washington offers many evocative symbols of democracy among its historic sites (not all of which are made of white marble). These are the main attractions for the eighteen million visitors who flock to the city each year.

Many of these structures are but a short walk away from each other on and around the Mall, the grassy expanse that serves as the centerpiece of Washington's grand design. The tall, graceful Washington Monument, rising 555 feet from the center of the Mall, remains the city's dominant landmark. On the Mall's west end is the shrinelike Lincoln Memorial; nearby, on the banks of the Tidal Basin, stands the Jefferson Memorial. In Constitution Gardens, a memorial of another sort, the black granite Vietnam Veterans Memorial, provides a sobering statement on war.

The Lincoln Memorial anchors the east-west axis of the Mall (inset previous page). Designed by Henry Bacon to memorialize Abraham Lincoln, the nation's sixteenth president, the Greek-style temple with Roman-style roof is a magnificent sight at all times, but it is especially impressive at dawn and dusk. Framed by fifty-four Ionic columns, the Jefferson Memorial (previous page), dedicated in 1943, was the last monument to be erected on the Mall. Inside the memorial is a nineteen-foot bronze statue of Thomas Jefferson, and inscribed on the walls are excerpts from his writings.

*T*he National Cathedral (above), ornamented by a George Washington statue, is run by the Episcopal church, but it opens its doors to worshippers of all denominations. The church is built in the shape of a cross, with twin towers in the west and a main tower in the center.

*D*uring a performance of Our American Cousin on April 14, 1865, while sitting in his box at Ford's Theatre, President Abraham Lincoln was shot by John Wilkes Booth. Restored in 1968, the theater now houses a museum of Lincoln memorabilia, where you can read the assassin's diary and see the pistol he used to kill Lincoln.

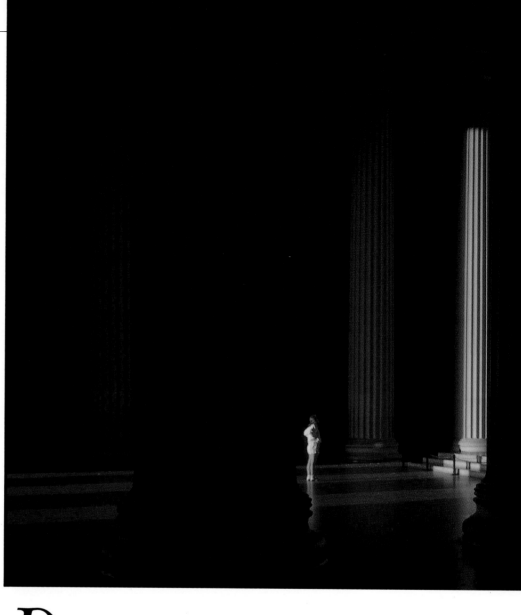

*D*aniel Chester French's statue of Lincoln is the Lincoln Memorial's centerpiece. It took sculptors four years to carve twenty-eight blocks of white Georgia marble into the nineteen-foot statue of a seated Lincoln gazing over the Reflecting Pool toward the Washington Monument and the Capitol. Inscribed on the Memorial's chamber are two of Lincoln's most impressive speeches: the Gettysburg Address and the Second Inaugural Address. One century after Lincoln's term, another great American rhetorician, Martin Luther King, Jr., inspired thousands of people in a speech from the steps of the Memorial as he told of his "dream."

Elsewhere in Washington are Ford's Theater, where President Lincoln was assassinated; the dramatic World War II Iwo Jima Memorial; the gothic National Cathedral; and, in nearby Arlington National Cemetery, the grave of John F. Kennedy and the Tomb of the Unknowns, where the changing of the military guard occurs like clockwork. There's certainly enough to keep the determined visitor scurrying about for weeks.

These monuments are part of Washington's lifeblood. Tourism is the city's second largest industry, and each year nearly $120,000 is allocated to a quarterly cleaning of Washington's fifty-six major statues and monuments. Considering the economic, historic, and aesthetic value of these structures, that may well be the most prudent government spending in history.

A *somber reminder of wartime atrocities, the Vietnam Veterans Memorial (above) is a V-shaped black granite wall listing the names of 58,132 Americans who died or were lost in the Vietnam conflict. An addition to the Vietnam Veterans Memorial wall (right) depicts three Vietnam servicemen. Since it was dedicated in November 1982, the Memorial, in the bucolic Constitution Gardens, has attracted thousands of visitors who come to pay respect to the many Americans who sacrificed their lives in the Vietnam War.*

*T*he graceful, domed Jefferson Memorial was designed by John Russell Pope in the Parthenon form that Jefferson followed in designing his home —Monticello — and the rotunda of the University of Virginia.

*S*ituated on the south shore of the Tidal Basin, the Jefferson Memorial was built on land reclaimed from the swampy edges of the Potomac River. When the 600 cherry trees that surround the Basin are in bloom, the Romanesque building and the lands, designed by noted landscape architect Frederick Law Olmsted, Jr., compose a picture-perfect scene.

*T*he Mall is the culmination of Washington's grand design. Studded with and surrounded by the Capitol building, Washington Monument, Library of Congress, and Smithsonian Museum, it is the main attraction for all visitors.

T*he Tomb of the Unknowns, for-*
merly the Tomb of the Unknown Sol-
dier, remains the biggest attraction at
nearby Arlington National Cemetery.
At all times, a soldier from the "Old
Guard" Third U.S. Infantry protects
the marble-block tomb and regularly
performs the precise heel-clicking,
salute-studded changing of the guard.

PART TWO

Occupational Washington

Nearly one-fourth of the people in the Washington area work for the Federal government, and another large portion work in related fields. Metropolitan Washington has the highest percentage of lawyers and psychiatrists in the country. Fifty out of every thousand Washingtonians are attorneys, many of whom write or interpret laws or lobby to change legislation; many of the psychiatrists are engaged in research.

Although administration–the production of words (spoken, on paper, in computers)– for the governing of more than 238 million U.S. citizens is a major industry, Washington is no different from the average large American city. The population of the metropolitan area, including the suburbs of Maryland and Virginia, is 3.5 million people, and those people work in an enormous variety of professions: from U.S. Supreme Court justices and Senators who work in gorgeous landmark buildings to Franciscan friars and academicians at the esteemed Georgetown University; from conductors on the ultra-efficient Metro transit system to diplomats and professional lobbyists who ride the trains daily.

The Supreme Court (previous page) meets from October through June to hear approximately 160 cases a year in a room with 150 seats available to the public. In the courtroom, the nine black-robed Justices listen to oral arguments and announce their rulings from high-backed leather chairs in front of heavy red velvet draperies. Washington–especially the area in front of the White House–naturally attracts more than its share of protestors (inset previous page), who feel it is their right to bring their complaints directly to the source.

*L*ike all major American cities, Washington has to contend with the usual

urban problems, such as traffic—which can be particularly heavy on the routes

that cross over the Potomac and Anacostia Rivers (above).

When the city's original planner, Pierre L'Enfant, looked upon Jenkins Hill—the area's highest point—in 1790, he saw a "pedestal waiting for a monument." The monument built there is the Capitol building, originally called Congress House, which continues today in its original function: as home to the Senate and House of Representatives.

*A*lthough it was virtually burned to the ground by British forces in 1812, the Capitol was rebuilt in time for President James Monroe to take the oath of office there in 1817. The building's architecture–including its magnificent dome–set the style for state capital buildings around the nation. Inside is the beautifully painted Rotunda–where the dome rises to 180 feet above the floor–and the original Congressional chambers.

*F*ive-point stars and the United States seal decorate the front gate of 1600 Pennsylvania Avenue, one of the world's most famous addresses. Inside the White House—home and office of the U.S. President—the furnishings change from administration to administration. However, the exterior has looked the same since the sandstone building was painted white to cover fire damage incurred during the War of 1812.

*T*he presidential inauguration ceremonies take place every four years on the steps of the Capitol. Here Franklin Delano Roosevelt calmed the fears of a Depression-era nation by declaring "The only thing we have to fear is fear itself," and John F. Kennedy began his presidency proclaiming, "Ask not what your country can do for you, ask what you can do for your country."

*T*he U.S. Treasury Building, built in 1842, is the oldest government department building. Legend has it that Andrew Jackson, impatient with the indecision of city planners, threw down his walking stick and declared that the Treasury would stand where the stick landed. As it happened, the Greek Revival building upset the original plan calling for a direct line from the Capitol to the White House, and now official parades must dogleg around the Treasury.

*T*he Supreme Court of the United States existed for 135 years before it was deemed worthy of its own home, a stunning neo-classic building constructed of the whitest marble fronted by Corinthian pillars. Designed by Cass Gilbert and completed in 1935, the Supreme Court Building resembles an ancient Greek temple.

33

*T*here is a wealth of military activity in the government city, as evidenced by frequent parades and the perfectly choreographed honor guard drills that the public can witness (right). Along with the Federal Government, the armed forces maintain a strong presence in Washington, and heavily decorated Special Forces Veterans of the U.S. Army remind others of the sucesses and sacrifices wars demand (above).

*E*mbassy Row (opposite page, top), stretching along both sides of a bend in Rock Creek, is the center of diplomatic life in Washington. The street is lined with more than 130 embassies from around the world, a different flag hanging in front of every building for blocks and blocks. Many of the embassies have moved into mansions built in the 1800s by the nation's industrial millionaires. Originally called the War, Navy, and State Building, the old Executive Office Building (opposite page, bottom) housed all three of these departments before the Pentagon was built. Patterned after the Louvre in Paris, it was the world's largest office building when it was completed in 1888. Today it houses a presidential suite and offices of the Vice President, Presidential assistants, and Presidential commissions. The Gothic spires of Georgetown University (above), the oldest Jesuit school in the U.S. (founded in 1789), lend a scenic, medieval look to the eastern bank of the Potomac River. In addition to fielding a power-house basketball team every year, Georgetown is one of the most prestigious academic institutions in the country.

When completed in the 1990s, the Metro will be one of the nation's most extensive and efficient urban transportation systems, with stations spread over one hundred miles. For Washingtonians, distant neighborhoods and parts of suburban Virginia and Maryland are now but a quick, clean, inexpensive ride away.

*T*he Metro, Washington's train system, is not called a subway because much of it is above ground. The underground stations, though, are relatively quiet, well lit, airy, climate-controlled, and aesthetically pleasing.

he Reflecting Pool captures the reflections of both the Washington Monument and the Lincoln Memorial. The idyllic setting has been the site of many celebrations and demonstrations, including the 1963 Civil Rights March on Washington.

*F*riar Cornelius Harper is one of the Order of the Friars Minor, resident acolytes and keepers of the beautiful grounds at the Franciscan Monastery (left), officially known as the Commissariat of the Holy Land for the United States. Among the many reproductions of Holy Land shrines at the Monastery are the Grotto of Bethlehem and the Holy Sepulcher, and underneath is a version of the Roman catacombs. The walls of the Islamic Center (above) are inlaid with turquoise and gold, and the rooms are furnished with the work of Middle Eastern artisans. This building serves as the cultural and religious hub for the staffs of the Islamic nations that maintain embassies in Washington.

*O*utside the President's Oval Office, colorful roses adorn the beautifully

manicured Rose Garden, an eighteenth century style garden planted in 1913 and

redesigned in 1962 at the request of John F. Kennedy.

*A*lthough construction of the White House began in 1792, the President's Palace–as it was called then–was not completely finished until Andrew Jackson moved in thirty-seven years later. The Georgian country house, designed by James Hoban, has been home to thirty-nine presidents and their families. The only United States president who did not reside there was George Washington, who served his term in Philadelphia while the capital city was being built.

PART THREE

Recreational Washington

For every monument and Federal edifice in Washington, there's a generous expanse of unspoiled nature offering a multitude of recreational opportunities. Rock Creek and Potomac Parks, the banks of the Potomac River, the National Arboretum, the C&O Canal towpath, and the National Zoo are just a few places to find relief from urban anxiety. They are also some of the best spots for a family picnic, as are the grounds of the city's historical attractions. Have lunch on a blanket under the shade of a blossoming cherry tree or in the shadow of the Washington Monument. Sometimes the street itself—especially in Georgetown and around Dupont Circle–is the center of activity, as people congregate to read, nap, sell wares, play chess, or trade gossip.

*E*verybody in Washington enjoys the weather in spring and fall (previous page), and the city's many parks offer all people–from office worker to street-dweller–a chance to escape temporarily from the urban hustle and bustle. The Capitol building stands atop the most prominent hill in Washington, and the best view of the city is afforded from its west side (inset previous page). Its extensive verdant grounds make an excellent location for a family picnic. The Potomac River runs from northwest to southeast through the heart of Washington, empty-ing into the Chesapeake Bay (above). For sport fishermen and seafood lovers, the river is more than just scenic; it is possible to catch all sorts of edible delights in the region's waters, including blue crabs, rockfish, oysters, and shrimp.

Of course, another popular activity is relaxing at home. Some of the area's residents are fortunate enough to live in magnificent Georgetown mansions, but for an enormous per-centage of the population, home means the ghettos of the southeast and northeast districts. Just a few blocks away from the shiny Capitol, these devastated neighborhoods are disturbing reminders of the city's—and country's—combina-tion of incredible wealth and great poverty.

But even the workers who devote them-selves to closing this economic rift try to forget the workaday world during their leisure time. Washington provides many opportunities to par-ticipate in other activities—a stroll, a boat ride, a scenic drive. In spring, when the weather is per-fect and the trees are in bloom, these are all pleasant reminders of a city designed nearly two centuries ago to rival in splendor the great capi-tals of Europe.

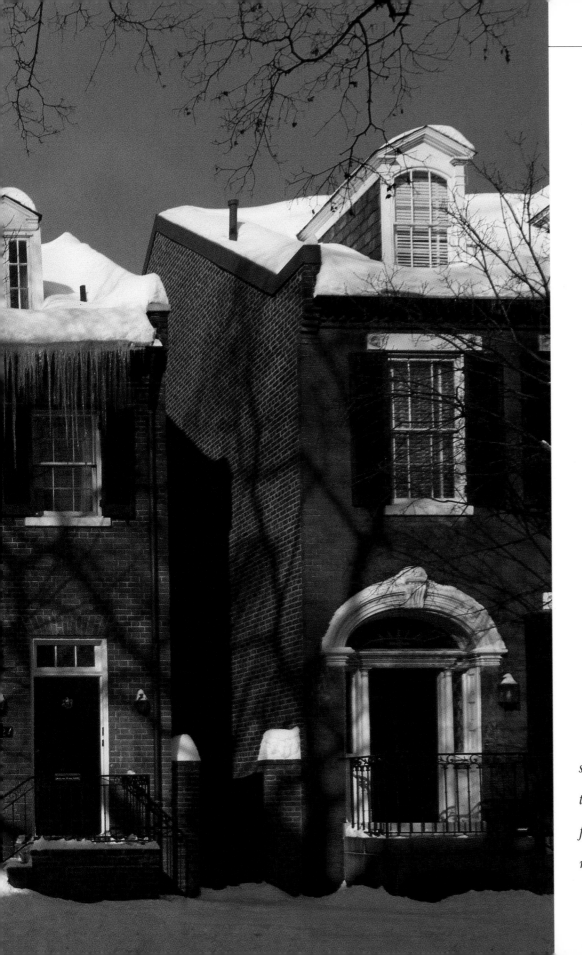

*T*hough it is easily forgotten during the sweltering summers, Washington does get its fair share of snow--though rarely in blizzard proportions. On crisp winter days, fresh white flakes and icicles form a pleasant contrast to the red brick townhouses of Georgetown.

*D*uring March and April, the U.S. Botanic Gardens offers an incredibly colorful display of azaleas. During other seasons, visitors flock to the cast-iron and glass Victorian greenhouse to gaze at orchids, Easter lilies, tulips, poinsettias, and chrysanthemums.

*E*ven the zoo in Washington is not free of politics. The two black-and-white panda bears are not only the most adorable animals in the National Zoological Park, but since they were given to the zoo in 1972 by the People's Republic of China, they have become a symbol of renewed positive relations between the United States and China.

*W*ashington is at its most beautiful in the spring, and the 444-acre National Arboretum is an unparalleled spot for strolling or relaxing among the blooming flowers and white and pink cherry blossoms. Established primarily as a place to conduct research on trees and shrubs, it remains one of the capital's loveliest locations.

*T*he capital's blossoming cherry trees are among the city's most famous annual attractions. Each April, Washington hosts a week-long Cherry Blossom Festival, which includes

a pageant, a parade, and the crowning of a Cherry Blossom Queen. Every year, festival organizers hope that the blossoming of the trees coincides with the dates of the festival.

*T*he natural sights of Washington can often rival the city's many monuments and historic buildings, especially during spring. The flowery banks of the Potomac suggest a life so peaceful and uncomplicated as to make it seem miles and miles from the center of government.

*D*upont Circle, a pleasant small park with a fountain in the center, offers a bit of green grass in an otherwise bustling area. Some come here to feed the squirrels and socialize, while others come to sit in the sun and relax.

56

*T*he grounds of the Washington Monument make for a great play area. On warm, breezy days, as the fifty American flags that surround the monument flap gently back and forth in the breeze, the large lawn has been known to play host to softball games, kite flying, and frisbee competitions.

*W*ashington is not without a sense of humor. Every year its overabundant pageantry and officialdom are mocked in the Gross National Parade (left), supported by the Paper Pushers Drill Team. Two young Washingtonians enjoy a spring day by the river in West Potomac Park (below), the public lands around the Tidal Basin and Lincoln Memorial.

*S*ome of the city's liveliest street activity occurs in the Dupont Circle neighborhood, which is made up of young couples gentrifying the area as well as members of the counter-culture left over from the 1960s and early 1970s.

*W*alking along the Potomac River, you can often hear the rhythmic chants of "Stroke-stroke-stroke" as oarsmen and women from local schools and clubs put their all into the graceful sport of crew.

Washington is incredibly livable, thanks to the many parks within the city limits. One of the favorite routes for runners is through West Potomac Park (inset), along the river under the trees. The area around the Tidal Basin (right) offers a pleasant escape from the city's cacophony. Among the park's recreational spaces is Lincoln Field, the site of fierce, picturesque polo matches.

*T*he old Chesapeake & Ohio (C&O) Canal stretches for 184 miles from Georgetown to Cumberland, Maryland. The tree-lined towpath is a favorite for strollers, joggers, and bicyclists. In the best preserved section of this late-eighteenth-century canal, parallel to the Potomac River in Georgetown, it is still possible to ride down the waterway on a mule-drawn boat.

*M*any of the city's most colorful characters hang out in the Dupont Circle

area, relaxing and chatting or selling their wares on the street—a vibrant street-life that

contrasts with the neighborhood's magnificently preserved nineteenth-century homes.

PART FOUR

Cultural Washington

Washington has always been a mecca of government and an essential tourist destination. Yet it took a generous gift and a lot of hard work to transform it into a cultural center with an incomparable cluster of museums and a busy schedule of world-class performing arts events.

In his will, British scientist James Smithson earmarked his fortune for the formation of an "establishment for the increase and diffusion of knowledge among men." Today the Smithsonian Institution's fourteen galleries and museums (eight of which are on the Mall) form the hub of the world's largest museum complex. Not only do the National Air and Space Museum, National Museum of Natural History, Hirshhorn Museum, National Portrait Gallery, and the others contain treasures ranging from the Wright

Designed by Edward Durrell Stone, the enormous Carrara-marble-faced Kennedy Center (previous page) holds an opera house, concert hall, and three theaters—for drama, cinema, and chamber music—in addition to three restaurants. On some nights, all five houses have performances. The National Gallery of Art (previous page, inset) maintains one of the world's most impressive collections of European and American art, from the works of the Old Masters to contemporary masterpieces—including the Ginevra de' Benci, *Leonardo da Vinci's only painting outside of Europe. The gallery's old Neoclassical building is connected to I.M. Pei's strikingly modern East Wing by an underground concourse.*

*O*verlooking the Potomac River, the John F. Kennedy Center for the Performing Arts, opened in 1971, helped solidify Washington's position as a cultural center. The building's Roof Terrace offers one of the best nighttime views of Washington, the Mall, and the river.

Brothers' 1903 flyer to several Andy Warhol paintings, but they have also led the way to a more cultured Washington where other spectacular museums, such as the National Gallery of Art, have been able to thrive.

With the opening of the John F. Kennedy Center for the Performing Arts in 1971, Washington was finally able to support a healthy lively arts scene. In five halls under one enormous roof, patrons can enjoy opera, drama, the National Symphony, dance, chamber music, and film.

And there's more. Wolf Trap Farm Park in nearby Virginia is the only national park dedicated to the performing arts. There are also smaller galleries and regional theaters and plenty of clubs with rock-and-roll and jazz. The Smithsonian and Kennedy Center are just the hubs from which cultural Washington continues to expand.

*T*he National Air and Space Museum, the Smithsonian's (and Washington's) most-visited museum, is a celebration of flight and a showcase for the history of aviation and space technology. Among its numerous treats is the Spirit of St. Louis—the plane Charles Lindbergh used in the first solo nonstop flight across the Atlantic Ocean—the Wright Brothers' 1903 flyer, and a wonderful film, To Fly.

*A*t the Capital Children's Museum (above), kids play and learn in an invaluable hands-on environment. There are ladders to climb, computers to use, and cars to drive. They can master the mass transit experience by play-riding in a bus or taxi, or explore other cultures by trying their clothes and sampling their food. The Arts and Industries Building (right), housing one of the world's largest collections of American memorabilia from the Victorian age, is just one of the Smithsonian Institution's fourteen treasure-stocked museums, galleries, and parks. At last count, the Smithsonian—which attracts more visitors than any other tourist center in the United States—contains more than thirty million catalogued items.